**Spiritual Warfare Ministries
Presents**

WHEN ALL HELL BREAKS LOOSE!

HOW TO WEATHER THE STORM

by Kenneth Scott

Scriptures in this publication are taken from the King James version of the Bible or paraphrased by the author.

When All Hell Breaks Loose

1st Printing

ISBN: 0-9667009-4-5

Copyright © 2002 by Kenneth Scott
Spiritual Warfare Ministries, Inc.
P.O. Box 2024
Birmingham, AL 35201-2024
(205) 853-9509

To request written permission to reproduce copies of sections of this publication, write to:

Spiritual Warfare Ministries
Attention: Kenneth Scott
P.O. Box 2024
Birmingham, Alabama 35201-2024

(205) 853-9509

Contents

Dedication

This book is dedicated to the memory of my late mother, Mrs. Inez Scott Miles, a loving mother, who I shall always love and cherish in my memories.

This book is also dedicated to my precious and wonderful wife, Doris, who has supported me through many of my trials and storms of life.

Preface

As a teacher and an evangelist, I love to teach the people of God how God wants to bless them with success and prosperity. I also love to preach and teach how God is well able to deliver His people from any situation. He is the Mighty God. He is greater and mightier than any power that comes against His people, and He is well able to deliver us from the hands of the enemy. But along with teaching God's people about His blessings, prosperity and deliverance, there's another message that must be taught. It's the message of the storm, and what to do in a storm.

It's a message that is not popular, because we hate to imagine ourselves going through the storm. But no matter how unpopular or undesirable this subject may be, the fact is—we will all face storms in our lives. But just as God is able to bless and prosper us, He is also able to strengthen us and take us through our storms of life, and come through as pure gold.

This book uses the same principles that are used to survive a natural storm, and parallels them with spiritual principles and concepts that will help you to come through your spiritual storms. You don't have to be a victim of the storm. If you apply these principles to your life, you too will be able to survive the storm, "When All Hell Breaks Loose."

When All Hell Breaks Loose

Introduction

Matthew 7:24-27 Therefore whosoever heareth these sayings of mine, and doeth them, I will liken him unto a wise man, which built his house upon a rock: and the rain descended, and the floods came, and the winds blew, and beat upon that house; and it fell not: for it was founded upon a rock. And every one that heareth these sayings of mine, and doeth them not, shall be likened unto a foolish man, which built his house upon the sand: And the rain descended, and the floods came, and the winds blew, and beat upon that house; and it fell: and great was the fall of it.

In this familiar passage of scripture, Jesus gives us a parable about two houses. One of them fell and the other did not. We know the obvious point that Jesus was making in this parable. It was the fact that the house that did not fall was built on the Rock and foundation of Jesus Christ, and the one that did fall was not.

We know that it was the lack of a stable, solid foundation that caused one of the houses to fall; but in this case we want to focus on the elements that caused it to fall. Although the inadequate foundations lead to its fall, it was ultimately the elements of the rains, floods, and winds that led to its demise.

These houses represent our lives. It is Satan's desire to make our houses fall. He uses the same spiritual elements of the rains, floods and winds to beat against our houses (our lives) in an attempt to get us to fall. In this book, we will learn how to survive the storm, and prevail, *"when all hell breaks loose."*

Chapter 1

The Elements

The Rains

R ains represent troubles in our lives. Many new Christian converts come to Christ only as a desperate attempt to put an end to their troubles they are experiencing. They think that once they come to Christ, all their troubles will be over. That's the farthest thing from the truth. In fact, God promised us that we would have trouble.

In Psalms 34:19, the bible says, *"Many are the afflictions of the righteous: but the LORD delivereth him out of them all."* God has never tried to lead us to believe that we would have a utopian experience in our walk with Him. He forewarned us of the battle to come. If you read the entire account of this passage in Matthew Chapter 26, you will find that the elements actually came against both houses.

The house that was built upon the right foundation was hit with the same calamities as the house built on the sand. The difference in the two houses was that one was able to weather the storm and the other was not. And, if you live long enough, your house will not be spared from the attacks of the enemy. However if you apply the right principles to your life, you too will be able to weather the storms in your life, "when all hell breaks loose."

Before we came to Christ, we were friends with Satan. Spiritually speaking, Satan was our father, and sin was our master. The only thing that kept most of us from being more deviant than we were as sinners, were the repercussions we could face as a result of our sins. Although we may not have been directly in opposition against God, and intentionally on Satan's side, because of our nature of sin, we were on Satan's side and enemies of God. We were also headed towards the same eternal destination and damnation of hell as Satan. But thank God for His mercy. It was through His mercy and grace through Christ that God derailed us from our certain path of hell's punishment and destruction, and re-routed our path to a new eternal destination of heaven and eternal glory.

When we opened our hearts and minds to receive Christ, we made a switch, and were instantly born into the family of God. At that time, we also instantly became enemies at war with Satan. If we have truly given Christ our hearts, Satan can no longer look forward to having us as his company in eternal hell. So, since he cannot take us to hell with him, his desire for our lives is to bring as much hell against us as he can right here on earth.

So again, the rains represent trouble. Trouble can come in many different facets of life. Troubles can range from something as small as a flat tire on your way to work, to problems in your marriage, finances or in any area.

Floods

The difference between spiritual rains and floods are the same difference between the physical or natural rains and floods. Floods come as a result of rain. The difference is that they are created only where there is an excess amount of rain that falls on one particular area at one time.

For example: If it down-poured six inches of rain over a period of one hour, it would probably overwhelm the city's sewage and drainage system and cause flooding. However, if that same amount of rain fell over a period of a week, it would probably not result in flooding, because the city's sewage system would have time to properly absorb and disperse that amount of rain over that period of time. It's the same in the spiritual realm. A spiritual flood arises when you experience an excess amount of trouble at one time in one particular area.

You might be able to easily deal with having problems with your car and spending several thousand dollars to repair it over a year's time. But imagine if you had to spend thousands of dollars and deal with eight or nine breakdown with your car within one month. If this happened within the course of one month, it would create all kinds of stress, frustration and other oppressive problems.

Just as the city's sewage system would be able to easily assimilate large amounts of rain over a longer period, our soul is better able to deal with trouble over longer periods. But when problems arise all at one time, they affect our soul, and many of us lose our faith and fall apart.

Some people see trouble in one's life as a sign that they are not living right and operating in sin and disobedience. Many times, trouble does not come upon us because we are in sin. Sometimes it comes because we are doing something right. As we all know, we are in a spiritual warfare. One of the strategies of warfare is that you focus your attacks on areas that cause the most difficulties. That's exactly what happens in the spiritual realm with many of us. It's because we have been praying, speaking the Word, and obeying God, that many attacks come upon us. The reason why Satan chooses to attack us is because we become serious threats to him and cause major problems for him in the spiritual realm. Satan's attack on Job's life was not a result of sin, but one of righteousness.

I often hear people say that they don't experience problems with Satan. If a person is living the true Christian life and doing what they should be doing, they should be causing some type of trouble for Satan in the spiritual realm. If they are, Satan will attempt to retaliate against them as a threat. But, if they are living the Christian life and there are no problems in their life anywhere, it could be very well that they are not a threat to Satan at all, and he is pleased having them right where they are.

Winds

The winds that Jesus is referring to in this passage are not average, everyday mild winds. They are super winds that are experienced in hurricanes and tornadoes. We said earlier that too much rain at one time makes a flood. So, if you get severe rains, flooding and these type of high destructive winds all at one time, you now have either a hurricane or a tornado.

The difference between a spiritual flood and a spiritual storm is that a flood is caused by an excessive amount of serious trouble in one area and at one time. A storm, however, is severe trouble, but in two or more areas at one time.

* **Note**: Certain adversities such as death of a close loved one, a divorce, the loss of a job, and other emotional catastrophes can be characterized as a storm rather than a flood, even though it may only be one occurrence or in one area.

It seems that my most effective messages have come out of experience. When I began writing this book, I had no idea that I would experience the type of storm that I have. My storm began in August of 2001. It began with the passing of my sister. We had developed an extremely close brother and sister relationship. But in August of 2001, she died of Leukemia. Four months later my brother-in-law, whom I was also close to and had lived with for three years during my childhood died of lung cancer. A few weeks later, my brother was hit with a life threatening illness. Three weeks later, my mother, whom I loved dearly, had a massive stroke and died one month later.

All this happened within a six-month period of time. I would barely have a chance to begin dealing with and absorbing one crisis before I was hit with another.

This was by far the worst storm of my life. I began writing this book in June of 2001, but it wasn't until February of 2002 that I finished it. It was my wife who brought to my attention that I had been writing a book about the storm while going through one. So the points that are brought out in this book are not simply from something I thought of or heard from someone, but are from experience.

The death of my mother was almost unbearable. It was already difficult enough dealing with the loss of my sister, my brother-in-law, and the physical crisis with my brother. But when my mother passed away, I nearly lost it. My mother and I have always been as close as a mother and son could get. So, when she passed, it almost paralyzed me. While in this storm, I reached a point to where I didn't want to talk to anyone. I canceled speaking engagements. I went into a moment of deep depression. I just wanted to sleep my life away. But instead of going over the edge, I began to cry out to the Lord.

I cried out to the Lord that I didn't know what was going on. I didn't understand it. I didn't feel that I had done anything to deserve it. I didn't know what to do. When I cried out to the Lord, He brought me right back to this book that I had began writing months earlier. It was then that I realized that I had to practice what I had taught and preached. I had to apply these same principles to my life.

As I went further into my storm, I actually had to rewrite this book because of my personal experiences I now had. The Lord gave me new instructions and insight on how to go through my storm. As I began applying these instructions to my life, the Lord poured in the oil and wine in my heart and my soul. Then, before I knew it, I was strengthened, encouraged, able to walk in His strength and peace, and ready to continue to do His work.

God wants to teach His people how to not only praise Him, love Him and passionately serve Him in the good times, but to still do it in the bad times—*"when all hell breaks loose."*

Chapter 2

The Purpose of the Storm

T he devil has several agendas for our lives. They are the same agendas that are practiced in a theater of war. Once a war has begun, the first agenda is to keep personnel and supplies from getting to the war zone. The next plan is, if possible, to destroy the enemy in occupied areas. The third focus is that if you cannot destroy them, try to neutralize them and their ability to fight, thereby minimizing their efforts and attacks against you.

Satan has the same agendas for us. He sends the rains, floods and winds against us to accomplish the same results. His first agenda is to keep us from receiving Christ and becoming born again. He leads us down the path of temptation and attempts to lure us away from going after God with the taste of sin. He uses sin and deception in an attempt to keep us from coming to God.

If he is not successful in keeping us away from God and receiving Christ, he goes to his next agenda—which is to destroy our lives. However, since God has His hand upon us, Satan is unable to destroy us. Therefore, since he is unable to destroy us, he then moves to his third agenda. This agenda is a three-fold agenda. The end result of each of these points is to neutralize us and our effectiveness against him. Satan's third agenda for us is as follows:

1. To get us to completely turn away from God and go back to serving sin.

2. To drain us of our spiritual strength and faith (to sift us as wheat).

3. To neutralize or hinder our desire to pray for and help others.

To Turn Us Away From God

Romans 8:35-39 Who (or what) *shall separate us from the love of Christ? Shall tribulation, or distress, or persecution, or famine, or nakedness, or peril, or sword? As it is written, for thy sake we are killed all the day long; we are accounted as sheep for the slaughter. Nay, in all these things we are more than conquerors through him that loved us. For I am persuaded, that neither death, nor life, nor angels, nor principalities, nor powers, nor things present, nor things to come, nor height, nor depth, nor any other creature, shall be able to separate us from the love of God, which is in Christ Jesus our Lord.*

In this passage, Paul is asking the question, "What will we allow to separate us from loving God?" He goes on to name many things, but concludes by saying that we should not allow any of them to separate us from loving God or turn our hearts away from Him.

Satan is after your love for God. Jesus said, "*Ye cannot*

serve two masters; you will either love one and hate the other." Jesus is telling us that there can only be one master of our soul—Jesus or Satan. Many people say that Jesus is Lord and master of their lives, but in actuality, Satan is the true master. If Satan can use the storms to turn or separate our passion and love for God, then he will be able to turn our hearts and love to something else (sinful things).

Satan uses the storms in an attempt to turn our love, heart and passion away from God. Unfortunately, there are many who (because of the pressures of the storm) turn away from God and turn to alcohol, drugs, sexual affairs, and other methods of escapism to get away from the stress of the storm. In the process of utilizing these detrimental methods, some are drawn down into the depths of spiritual bondage and are held captive and bound by demonic stronghold spirits. Some never recover from this depth of satanic bondage and spend the remainder of their lives in the spiritual *hog's pen.*

To Sift Us As Wheat

Secondly, if Satan cannot turn our hearts away from God, and get us to sink into his spiritual bondage, his next desire is to rob us of our heart and passion for God.

Luke 22:31-32 "And the Lord said, Simon, Simon, behold, Satan hath desired to have you, that he may sift you as wheat: But I have prayed for thee, that thy faith fail not..."

Jesus forewarned Peter of Satan's plan of attack against him. Because God's hand was upon Peter, Satan could not destroy his life. Since he could not destroy his life, Satan's next plan of attack was to attempt to sift the very life of God out of him.

This sifting is like the sifting of a spider. When a spider catches its prey (lets say that it's a fly), the spider first paralyzes the fly with its venom. The spider does not eat the fly all at once. It wraps the fly in its cocoon and returns periodically to eat of the fly until it is consumed. The way that a spider eats its victim is from the inside out. If you were to see the fly in the spider's web, it would look like the fly is fully intact. But the only thing that the spider actually leaves of its victim is the shell. It may look like the fly is whole, but the spider has consumed the insides (life) of the fly, leaving only the appearance (the shell) of the fly.

This is the goal of Satan for every born-again Christian. He uses the storms of life to get us into his web—the place of despair, hopelessness and depression. Depression is a spirit that works like a spider's web. It's a spirit that paralyzes a person to such a degree that it oppresses their will to press forward. If it is not dealt with, this spirit will cause a (once passionate and fiery) Christian to loose their passion for God.

While a person is trapped in this web of depression, Satan drains them of their joy (which is our strength). It leaves them not wanting to pray, praise and worship God, attend church, read and study His Word, or anything else which lifts us up and gives us encouragement.

The longer a person is held in the cocoon of depression from the storm, the more Satan will drain the life of God out of them. They may come to church and appear to carry on their normal routine for an outward show, but it's only a shell; inwardly they are empty.

Peter was being used greatly by God. Peter's fire and boldness through Christ caused havoc for Satan in the spiritual realm. Satan knew that if Peter kept this trend, he would cause devastating damage against his kingdom of darkness. Satan's plan was to use the storm to do this sifting. His plan was to destroy Peter and his testimony— leaving him as a shell of a man who once had a passion for God. Fortunately, because Jesus prayed and interceded for Peter, Satan's plan failed, and Peter rebounded from his failure and spiritual plunge and became a mighty man of God who was used greatly by the Lord.

Although Satan's plan failed against Peter, he has used it against many Christians throughout the ages. His desire is to get us in the storm, and sift the very life of God out of us. This state of spiritual emptiness is known in the Word of God as being Lukewarm.

Revelation 3:15-16 I know thy works, that thou art neither cold nor hot: I would thou wert cold or hot. So then because thou art lukewarm, and neither cold nor hot, I will spue thee out of my mouth.

God hates lukewarm Christians. Lukewarm Christians are those whose lives are so neutral and spiritually passive, that it is hard to tell that they are Christians. They say they are saved and born again, but they have little or no fruit to show it. No one knows they are Christians. They may go to church, but after they leave the church building, they also leave their Christianity and Christian walk right there.

They rarely pray. They rarely witness or tell anyone about the Lord. They have no real, true conviction for anything. They don't have a real passion for any of the things of God. Even though they confess to be on the Lord's side, they are ineffective for the Kingdom of God. And, since they are ineffective for the Kingdom of God, they are also ineffective against the kingdom of darkness.

There have been Christians that I have known whom at one time had a passion and fire for the Lord. However, because of the web of the storm in their lives, they spiritually digressed to a point to where you could barely tell they were still a Christian.

To Hinder Us From Praying For and Helping Others

The third thing that Satan wants to do is to minimize our prayer life for others. During the storm, most people are so overwhelmed with their own problems, that if they do pray, they spend all their time and efforts of prayer on themselves. If Satan can get us backed up in a corner like this, he has been successful in neutralizing our attacks against him in helping others.

Chapter 3

Recognizing the Storm

W hen most people enter a storm, when they do pray, they have a tendency to immediately blame the devil for their troubles and attempt to combat him with the Word. But before we can combat the devil, we must first come to recognize the type of storm in which we are engaged.

We must come to recognize the type of catastrophe we are in, if we are to survive it. If there is a danger of flash flooding, the reaction is different than that of a hurricane. If we react in a hurricane like we would in a flash flood, we could perish. With that in mind, the knowledge of what type of storm or catastrophe we are in is essential to our survival. Likewise, in the spiritual realm, when we are faced with a storm, we must also find out what kind of storm of adversity we are facing.

Psalms 139:23-24 Search me, O God, and know my heart: try me, and know my thoughts: and see if there be any wicked way in me.

In this passage, David asked God to search him and see if there was anything he had done wrong to cause this storm he was experiencing. David wanted to know if he had brought this storm upon himself, or was it simply an outright attack from the devil. Likewise, when storms of life come upon us, we need to do the same thing. When all hell breaks loose in our lives, we need to also search our hearts, seek the face of God, and find the reason for the attack.

Persecution Verses Prosecution

Persecution

We must determine whether our storm is a storm of "**Persecution**" or "**Prosecution**." Let's begin with understanding Persecution. Persecution is the evil, wrong, or injustice one receives as a direct result of their righteous or just actions, words or deeds.

For example: Job was persecuted (attacked by Satan), not because he had done anything wrong, but because he was a righteous and just man. Likewise, in our lives, there are times when we are attacked (go through the storm) even though we have not done anything wrong. It is just an outright attack from the enemy.

If it's a storm of persecution, we combat the devil's attack by speaking and praying the authority of God's Word. We will talk more in depths about this later. In a court of law, if a person is innocent of a crime, they present their evidence, and the law uses the evidence to declare their innocence. When we have allowed the Holy Spirit to search our hearts, and we resolve that it is an outright attack against us, and not because we have done anything wrong, then we stand on the law and evidence of the Word of God.

Prosecution

On the other hand, we can also have a storm of **prosecution**. We said that persecution is the wrong, evil or injustice someone receives because of the right they've done. Prosecution on the other hand, is the right (deserved) punishment someone receives because of the wrong they've done.

We blame many things on the devil for which he is not at fault. For example, the trouble we may be experiencing on our job may not be solely a result of the devil's attack, but because we may have been habitually late for work, or simply not doing our job properly. The trouble we may be experiencing in our finances could be caused by wasting, or mismanagement of our money, rather than the devil's attack.

Negligence

Many attacks upon our lives are a result of us being negligent, lethargic and apathetic in our Christian walk. It is also when we become careless and fail to keep watch and guard our lives and our homes from the relentless attacks of the enemy.

The prayer life of many Christians is sporadic and undisciplined. Many Christians pray by emotions and time opportunity rather than by discipline and priority. If we used the same discipline and priority of prayer that we do in eating, most of us would starve to death.

For example, there are days that we wake up late for work and do not have time to eat breakfast. During that same day, we may even have business to take care of during our lunch time and not have time to eat lunch. However, at some point during that day, we will find time to eat. It may be while we are on break at work. It may be while driving our car from one place to another. It could be anytime, but eventually we will make time to eat during the day.

Using the same example, let's say that we wake up late for work and miss our usual prayer time. Most Christians would just simply omit that day of prayer. But just as we would make time during that day to eat, we must also have the same mind to make time to pray. If we miss our usual morning time of prayer, we should not totally omit prayer for that day. We must also find time to pray. We may need to pray on our way to work. We may need to take our lunch hour to pray. We must be disciplined in prayer, that just as we would make time to eat if we had not eaten, to have that same determination to also make time for prayer.

Once we miss a day of prayer, it becomes easier to miss prayer the next day. Then before we know it, it's Friday, and we haven't prayed since Monday. During those days that we do not pray, we leave our lives and our family's lives uncovered, while giving Satan an opportunity to advance upon us.

Many times people blame the devil for the attack, when it is really not Satan's fault. Sometimes it's essentially our fault, and the problem should actually lie in us being negligent in our prayer life.

Some time ago, my wife and I were preparing to go on a vacation. We had planned to pack the car that evening, so all we had to do the next morning was to grab a few things and go. However, before I finished, while I was in the car, my wife came and told me that I had received a very important phone call for which I had been waiting. I took the call and forgot that I was loading the car.

The next morning, as I was bringing the last of the things to the car, it hit me like a ton of bricks, that I had left the car unlocked, the windows down, and my tape player in plain view for anyone to steal. And, sure enough, the next morning when I came to the car, my hand-held cassette stereo had been stolen. But I didn't get angry with the unknown thief who stole it; they were only doing what a thief does—steal. Instead, I got angry with myself for being negligent.

It's the same with us. Many Christians try to blame the devil for coming against them, when in fact, they are spiritually just as negligent as I was in leaving my car unsecured. And, just as I couldn't blame the thief, many Christians cannot blame the spiritual thief—the devil. He is just doing his job, which is taking advantage of our negligence. So, when we search our hearts, we must make sure that we are not the blame for leaving our lives, our family's lives and our home unguarded and unsecured by not being disciplined in prayer.

Sin and Disobedience

One reason for spiritual prosecution is as a result of our negligence. Another reason for spiritual prosecution is sin, unrighteousness and disobedience. We all know that Jesus Christ died on the cross that we might have eternal life. If we have received Christ into our hearts, we are saved and on our way to heaven. However, while we are here in the earth realm, we can allow sin and disobedience to rob us of the blessings of the Lord.

When we walk in continual sin, disobedience and un-righteousness, we spiritually let our hedge down, and open the door for Satan to have access into our lives. Even though we may be praying the Word of God over our lives (building up our hedge), continual sin counteracts our prayer and spiritually lowers the hedge—allowing Satan to come against us.

Are All Storms Sent By Satan?

Most of us assume that anytime we have gone through a storm that it was sent by Satan; but there are times when God sends the storms our way. However, God's purpose for sending the storms is different than that of Satan. Again, Satan's purpose is to ultimately destroy us or neutralize us. God's purpose is to get us to repent and change.

Jonah 1:1-4 Now the Word of the LORD came unto Jonah the son of Amittai, saying, arise, go to Nineveh, that great city, and cry against it; for their wickedness is come up before me. But Jonah rose up to flee unto Tarshish from the presence of the LORD, and went down to Joppa; and he found a ship going to Tarshish: so he paid the fare thereof, and went down into it, to go with them unto Tarshish from the presence of the LORD. But the LORD sent out a great wind into the sea, and there was a mighty tempest in the sea, so that the ship was like to be broken.

Jonah 1:17 Now the LORD had prepared a great fish to

swallow up Jonah. And Jonah was in the belly of the fish three days and three nights.

Jonah 2:1-3 Then Jonah prayed unto the LORD his God out of the fish's belly, and said, I cried by reason of mine affliction unto the LORD, and he heard me; out of the belly of hell cried I, and thou heardest my voice. For thou hadst cast me into the deep, in the midst of the seas; and the floods compassed me about: all thy billows and thy waves passed over me.

Jonah 2:9 But I will sacrifice unto thee with the voice of thanksgiving; I will pay that that I have vowed. Salvation is of the LORD.

In this familiar biblical account, God told Jonah to go to Nineveh and prophesy the Word of the Lord to the Ninevites. Instead, in his disobedience, Jonah boarded a ship to go to Tarshish. But notice above in verse four who sent the storm. It wasn't the devil that sent the storm—it was God.

Even though God sent the storm, His purpose for the storm was different than that of Satan. Again, Satan sends the storm to destroy us and to move us into disobedience and sin—away from the will of God. However, God sends the storm to get us to repent of our disobedience and sin, and to bring us back into His will.

In Chapter 2:1-3, you find Jonah finally repenting and crying out to the Lord. In verse 9, Jonah not only repented, he also had a change of heart and mind, and now desired to do the will of God. The end result of God sending the storm for Jonah wasn't destruction, but repentance, change and deliverance.

Likewise, in our lives, there are some storms that come upon us which are not sent by Satan, but by God. Like Jonah, there are times that it takes us going through the storm and getting in an uncomfortable place before we come to a place of repentance, and become open to hear and obey the voice of the Lord. I have people call all the time, often asking me to agree with them in prayer to prevent someone from going to prison. One of the first questions I always ask them is this: "is the person saved and born again?" I ask this because God is more interested in a person's soul and eternal destination than He is in them being uncomfortable for a period of time.

If a person is in rebellion to God and His Word, we have to sometimes allow them to get to a hard place before they become willing to repent and change. Due to our love for our family members and loved ones, we often get in the way and hinder the will of God to change their hearts. When we are praying for the souls of our loved ones, we have to sometimes say, "Lord, whatever you have to do to save them, do it!" It's a prayer that we don't want to pray because we don't want hardship to come upon them; but it's also a prayer that is sometimes necessary to pray if they continue in rebellion against God.

Jesus said in Matthew 16:26, *"For what is a man profited, if he shall gain the whole world, and lose his own soul?"* God loves them so much that He would rather allow adversity to come against them for a season and give them eternal life in glory, than to bail them out of adversity and have them spend eternity in hell. Prison has changed the hearts of many people. It becomes a place like Jonah's whale—a place for them to sit and realize their mistakes, sins and errors. And, like Jonah, it also becomes a place which brings them to true repentance and, thus bend their will towards God.

What Do We Do If It's a Storm of Prosecution?

What do we do if we determine that it is a storm of prosecution? Remember the criminal. Again, if he is innocent, he presents his evidence and the law declares him innocent. But on the other hand, it may be a case where the criminal is "guilty as sin," as they say. He may have been caught on video, had an eyewitness to the crime, or other overwhelming incriminating evidence against him. In this case, the law works against him because the evidence proves his guilt. In fact, in this case, the criminal would not even want to present a case at all. The reason is because the same law that would set him free and release him if he was innocent, is the same law that will send him to jail now that he is guilty. A person who is guilty beyond the shadow of a doubt has to approach the court and judge in an entirely different way than someone who is innocent.

What does the criminal do when he knows he is guilty and there's no way out? He falls upon the mercy of the court. He stands before the judge and the judge asks him, "How do you plea?" He then replies, "Guilty your honor." He does not attempt to present any evidence. In fact, if he tried to take his case to trial instead of admitting his guilt, his punishment could be far worse than if he had simply admitted his guilt from the beginning. When a guilty party falls upon the mercy of the court, the court is (most of the time) more lenient in giving its judgment or punishment, and will often allow some sort of plea-bargaining.

What do we do when we are going through a storm and we have searched our hearts, and the Holy Spirit reveals that the problem is with us—prosecution, not persecution? We do the same thing the criminal does when he is guilty beyond a shadow of a doubt. But instead of falling on the mercy of the court, we fall upon the mercy of God.

When David committed adultery with Bathsheba and God exposed his sins through the prophet Nathan, David did not try to defend himself with God. He made no attempts to declare what God's Word says or to remind God of His promises.

Just as the law would declare the criminal guilty and send him to jail if he was guilty, when we are guilty, the law (Word of God) also declares us guilty and worthy of God's punishment. So instead of David rehearsing the law (Word of God), he did like the criminal, and fell upon the mercy of God. This is where we get Psalms 51. It is the psalm of repentance and cry for mercy that David wrote after his sins with Bathsheba had been exposed.

Psalms 51:1-4 Have mercy upon me, O God, according to thy lovingkindness: according unto the multitude of thy tender mercies blot out my transgressions. Wash me thoroughly from mine iniquity, and cleanse me from my sin. For I acknowledge my transgressions: and my sin is ever before me. Against thee, thee only, have I sinned, and done this evil in thy sight...

Psalms 51:6-12 Behold, thou desirest truth in the inward parts: and in the hidden part thou shalt make me to know wisdom. Purge me with hyssop, and I shall be clean: wash me, and I shall be whiter than snow. Make me to hear joy and gladness; that the bones which thou hast broken may rejoice. Hide thy face from my sins, and blot out all mine iniquities. Create in me a clean heart, O God; and renew a right spirit within me. Cast me not away from thy presence; and take not thy holy spirit from me. Restore unto me the joy of thy salvation; and uphold me with thy free spirit.

After being exposed, David did not try to play dodge ball with God about his sins. He did not try to speak God's Word and remind God of what His Word says. Like the criminal, the Word would have declared his guilt. So he humbled himself before the great Judge of heaven and fell upon God's mercy. Likewise, if we search our hearts before the Lord and find that we are guilty—whether it is negligence, sin or disobedience, we also need to learn to fall upon the mercy of God.

The Bible says that God is rich in mercy. To be rich simply means that you have an overabundance of something. So when the Bible says that God is rich in mercy, it means that He has an overabundance of mercy.

Too often we associate the need for repentance with someone who has backslidden or gone astray from God. If we have been caught in the noose of Satan and drawn away from God, once the Holy Spirit is finally able to deal with our hearts, we should have a heart of repentance. Repentance is not something for sinners; it's something for all of us. It's something we should do every day.

In the Lord's Prayer, Jesus taught the disciples basic principles of prayer they were to pray about each day. One of the things He instructed them to do each day was to pray that God would *"forgive them of their debts"* (sins and transgressions). There are many types of prayers. One of them is the prayer of repentance. This is a time of prayer each day that we are to search our hearts and allow the Holy Spirit to deal with us and speak to us about our sins. If we ask God to search our hearts, He will. And He will also show us the error of our ways. The question is not whether or not God will show us our sins. The real question is, when He does, will we repent and get deliverance from them? This is something that we should do each day.

God is not looking for perfect people. He is simply looking for honest people. He knew that we would not be perfect. That's why He had to send Jesus Christ into the world to die for our sins. However, when we have committed and walked in the way of sin and transgressions, and the Holy Spirit speaks to our hearts about our sins, He is looking for us to be truthful, repent of them, and seek deliverance.

What often happens is that we ignore the voice of the Holy Spirit and refuse to repent. Instead of us admitting our negligence, sins or disobedience, we often attempt to justify ourselves in our own heart. When we fail to hear the voice of God calling for us to repent and change, God has to sometimes remove His hand from our lives. He has to sometimes allow calamity or despair to come upon us so that we can realize and recognize that we have sinned, been disobedient, or have missed God in some way, and seek His face for forgiveness and deliverance.

David knew that he had been living in sin with Bathsheba. I believe that God spoke to David through His Spirit many times to get him to repent and change his ways.

However, it wasn't until the Prophet Nathan came and exposed David and pronounced judgment upon him that he actually repented and changed. Likewise, with us, there are many times that we have done wrong, and it is not until God removes His hand from our lives and allows calamity to hit us, that we become open to the voice of God, and willing to repent and change.

We need to live a repented life each day. We do this by daily searching our hearts, allowing God to show us our sins, repenting of them, and seeking His face for deliverance. If we do this daily, we could avoid many pitfalls, disasters and storms in our lives.

Petitioning God for Mercy

There was a gentile woman who came and petitioned Jesus to deliver her daughter by casting a devil out of her. Prior to Jesus dying on the cross, the Jews were the only people who had a right to the promises of God. The law was, at that time, a physical law, and the physical Jews (descendants of Abraham) were the only ones who could inherit the promises of God. After Jesus came and died on the cross, He adopted us into the family of God, and we became the spiritual children of Abraham and, therefore, inheritors of the promise.

When she came seeking Jesus to deliver her daughter, at first, He ignored her. He ignored her because He knew that she was a Gentile, and had no right to the things of God. Finally, through her persistence, Jesus answered and told her that He was only sent to those who had a covenant with God.

Matthew 15:25-26 Then came she and worshipped him, saying, Lord, help me. But he answered and said, It is not meet to take the children's bread, and cast it to dogs.

Look at what Jesus said here. He referred to the blessings of God as *"the children's bread."* In other words, Jesus was saying that the blessings of healing, health, deliverance, prosperity and many other blessings belong to us as children of God. We have a right to them. However, He was also making it plain to her, that as a Gentile, she didn't have a right to the blessings of God. He even referred to her as a dog. When Jesus referred to her as a dog, He was not trying to degrade her as a human being; but the Bible regards those who are followers of God in high esteem. While at the same time, it refers to those who are not followers of God as infidels, dogs and many other derogatory names.

Matthew 15:27-28 And she said, truth, Lord: yet the dogs eat of the crumbs which fall from their master's table. Then Jesus answered and said unto her, O woman, great is thy faith: be it unto thee even as thou wilt. And her daughter was made whole from that very hour.

At first, she came pretending to be a Jew when she said, *"Have mercy on me, O Lord, thou son of David."* This was a term used by the Jews to specifically identify that person. So in essence, she was trying to act like she was a Jew, hoping that Jesus would not recognize her as a gentile.

After being exposed and acknowledging that she was out of covenant, this gentile woman responded with a profound statement. She said, *"Truth, Lord* (that as a gentile she did not have a right to or deserve the gifts of God), *yet the dogs eat of the crumbs which fall from their masters table."*

With this statement, she was acknowledging who she was (a Gentile, with no rights to the blessings of God), and the fact that she wasn't worthy to receive His blessings. With this statement, she was also acknowledging that God was the God of the universe with all power, authority and riches, and that God (the Master) has an abundance of everything.

She was comparing God's abundant blessings to the king's feasts. During those days, kings often held feasts to celebrate special holidays, occasions and victories. There was such an overwhelming abundance of food at the king's feasts, that there was always something falling on the ground. And, if you have ever had any pets around the house such as dogs, then you know that they are always right there ready to quickly eat up whatever falls to them on the floor. And, even though that meal may not have been prepared for the dog, it was such an overwhelming, over-abundance of food, that the dog became a primary beneficiary of something which was not originally intended for him.

This woman was in essence, telling Jesus that God is so great (or has such a smorgasbord) of riches and mercy, that even though she was like a dog, (undeserving of the blessings of God), to let her just partake of the crumbs (the excess) that fall. With this, she was also saying that as great as God is and as great as His power is, that the (power) of the Master's crumbs were more than enough to deliver her daughter.

With her faith, she tapped into the over-abundant mercy of God. God is so rich in mercy, that even though she did not deserve to receive this deliverance for her daughter, she received it anyway because she fell upon the mercy of God. Likewise, even when we are in the wrong, if we learn how to repent and fall upon God's mercy, He will not only defend us when we are right, but will also have mercy upon us, forgive us, help us, and deliver us, even when we are in the wrong and don't deserve it.

All of us have *sinned and come short of the glory of God*. All of us have *missed the mark* and have disobeyed the voice of God at times. But unlike Satan, God wants the storms to bring us closer to Him. God is not looking to hurt or destroy us with the storm, but to help us.

If you find yourself in a storm of prosecution, don't try to present your case by attempting to justify yourself or declare what God's Word says, just fall upon the mercy of God. Admit your guilt, sin or negligence. Cry out to Him for mercy, forgiveness and grace. Let Him know how sorrowful you are for disobeying Him or straying away. When you learn the ministry and prayer of repentance, you will find, like the Gentile woman, that God is rich and abundant in mercy. And, that He will not only help you when you are in the right, but (if you fall upon the mercy of the court), He is also willing to have mercy upon you and help you when you are guilty and undeserving of His mercy.

There are two prayers in the book, "The Weapons of Our Warfare, Volume 1," that will aid and assist you in this area. They are *"A Prayer when you have sinned,"* and *"A Prayer of the 51ˢᵗ Psalm."*

Chapter 4

Hide Yourself

W e have discovered that the first thing we do if we find ourselves in the midst of a storm is to determine in what type of storm we are caught. We must determine whether it is a storm of persecution or a storm of prosecution. We then act accordingly.

After we have identified what type of storm we are experiencing, and we have acted accordingly, we then go to the next step, which is to hide ourselves.

Job 1:13-19 And there was a day when his (Job's) sons and his daughters were eating and drinking wine in their eldest brother's house: And there came a messenger unto Job, and said, The oxen were plowing, and the asses feeding beside them: And the Sabeans fell upon them, and took them away; yea, they have slain the servants with the edge of the sword; and I only am escaped alone to tell thee. While he was yet speaking, there came also another, and said, The fire of God is fallen from heaven, and hath burned up the sheep, and the servants, and consumed them; and I only am escaped alone to tell thee. While he was yet speaking, there came also another, and said, The Chaldeans made out three bands, and fell upon the camels, and have carried them away, yea, and slain the servants with the edge of the sword; and I only am escaped alone to tell thee. While he was yet speaking, there came also another, and said, Thy sons and thy daughters were eating and drinking wine in their eldest brother's house: And, behold, there came a great wind from the wilderness, and smote the four corners of the house, and it fell upon the young men, and they are dead; and I only am escaped alone to tell thee.

This passage shows Job experiencing a tremendous storm in his life. Remember, we said earlier that a storm is a combination of several severe problems at or around the same time. This is what Job experienced. It seemed that before Job could catch his breath and absorb one crisis, he was hit with yet another. Before he knew it, Job had been hit with several catastrophes at the same time.

Job 1:20 Then Job arose, and rent his mantle, and shaved his head, and fell down upon the ground, and "worshipped".

This scripture shows us the first thing Job did after he was hit with the storm. He immediately fell upon the ground and *"WORSHIPPED"* God.

What do you turn to when all hell breaks loose in your life? If you are caught in a natural storm and do not seek some type of shelter, you will be severely injured or consumed by the storm. Likewise, in the spiritual realm, if you do not seek some type of shelter in the spiritual storm, you may also become spiritually, physically or emotionally injured or consumed.

Many make the mistake of seeking shelter from their storms in alcohol, drugs, sex and elicit affairs, and many other forms and methods of escapism from their troubles. However, the problem with these forms of escape is that after the intoxication wears off, the affects of the drugs wear off, and after the affair is over, the problems are still there staring them in the face. They may have escaped the reality of their problems for a few moments, but afterwards, the problems are still there and they still have to deal with them. What Job did in the midst of his storm was to hide himself from the effects and pressures of his storm by turning to God and worshipping Him.

1 Corinthians 10:13 There hath no temptation taken you but such as is common to man: but God is faithful, who will not suffer you to be tempted above that ye are able; but will with the temptation also make "a way to escape," that ye may be able to bear it.

In this passage, the word "temptation" is not temptation as in being lured to do something evil. This word temptation means a test, trial, or storm. So what this passage is actually saying is this:

There is no storm that shall come upon you that others have not commonly gone through. But God is faithful, who will not allow you to go through a storm above that you are able to bear; but in the midst of the storm, He will also make a way of escape for you. He will strengthen you and give you peace so that you will be able to handle the pressures of the storm.

The escape this passage is referring to is not necessarily an escape out of your troubles, but rather, an escape through your troubles. When we experience troubles in our lives, we want God to immediately take us out of our troubles. There are times when He will, but there are also times when God will take us through them. When He does, He will always give us the inner peace and strength we need to *"be able to bear it"* (handle the stress and pressures of the storm).

In the 23rd Psalm, David said, *"Yea, though I walk 'through' the valley..."* There are times when we must go through our valleys or storms. We know that God said that we can speak to our mountains, but He never said for us to speak to a valley. When you are going through the storm, He will make a way of escape for you. But again, the escape He is referring to is not necessarily an escape out of your storm, but sometimes an escape through your storms.

In 2 Corinthians Chapter 12, Paul sought the Lord three times for deliverance from a situation in his life. Finally, the answer came to Paul from God. God's answer to Paul was, *"My grace is sufficient for thee."* In other words, God was telling Paul that He was not going to take the problem or trouble away from Paul, but God was going to empower him with the strength of the Holy Spirit to go through his troubles.

When we cry out to God for help in a time of trouble, there are times that He will help us and deliver us out of the trouble. But, there are also times that God will not take us out of our trouble, but (like Paul) give us the strength to go through the storm or trouble.

We like to hear about how *God is a very present help*

in times of trouble. We like to hear that, "*Many are the afflictions of the righteous, but the Lord delivereth him from them all*." We love hearing and quoting scriptures like these, which promise God's hand of deliverance for us. But what we don't want to hear is how that God is able to take us through the valley or storm. We don't want to hear it because we don't like to think of actually having to go through a storm. As much as we hate to face it, the fact is that all of us will go through some kind of storm in life. There will be some storms we face that we won't be able to speak to and command to be removed. There are some storms that we will just have to go through.

I love to hear pastors and ministers speak of how God will bless us and prosper us. I think that we should be taught about the prosperity and blessings of the Lord. But I also feel that it's an injustice to the people of God if a pastor never teaches his people how to prevail in the storms of life. Because no matter who we are, how good we are, how righteous or holy we are, or how much we speak the Word of God, we will all have to go through some kind of storm.

Having to go through a storm is the bad thing. The good thing is, that *God's grace is sufficient for us* (to take us through). And just as He is able to bless and prosper us, that same grace and anointing is able to strengthen us, keep us, and empower us to make it through the storm.

Finding Shelter

In a natural storm, the first thing you do is to find shelter. This is exactly what Job did. He did not find his shelter in an alcohol bottle, with drugs, or in an affair. He found his shelter in worshipping the Lord. When we begin to turn to the Lord and worship Him, He begins to engulf us in Himself. Although we may be still going through the midst of the trouble or storm, He will begin to insulate us from the pressures and internal destructive effects of the storm. If we learn how to seek His shelter in the midst of our storms, He will begin to give us a peace in our hearts, as well as the mental, emotional and spiritual strength and stamina we need to endure the storm.

There are many who are consumed by the effects of the storm. We have all heard of millionaires, movie stars, sports stars, and other well-known celebrities who have committed suicide. People who commit suicide and drug overdoses are looking for shelter from their storm. They've tried all the forms of shelter they know of, but resolved that suicide was their only way out. When we hear of cases like these, we always wonder, "why would they commit suicide when they had so much going for them?" It's because they could not handle the effects of their storm.

Many of us have also known people who have had a nervous breakdown because of a storm. There are also a great deal of people who may not have suffered obvious outward destructive manifestations of the storm, but were left emotionally or mentally scarred from the storm for the remainder of their lives.

I've known people who went through a difficult, disheartening divorce at a young age, and were never able to open their hearts and love or trust anyone again. We've all seen on the 6:00 evening news where individuals have been fired from their job of many years, and went on a rampage shooting and killing innocent people on that job, then killing themselves. I've heard of a study about homeless people which states that over forty percent of homeless people in America are not homeless because they cannot find help or work, but because of some kind of emotional hurt or injury they experienced in life. These, and many other tragedies, have robbed people of the abundant life that God meant for them to have. They are people who are casualties of the storms of life. They are people who— because they didn't have a relationship with God, did not know how to get the proper shelter from the spiritual and emotional effects of the storm.

God tells us in Psalms 91 ***"He that dwelleth in the secret place of the Most High shall abide under the shadow of the almighty."*** That secret place He is referring to is a place of intimate worship.

To get to this secret place, you must make time to worship God. You have to get along with Him and lift up your hands and praise God. You begin to magnify Him, glorify Him, exalt Him and lift Him up. You begin to tell Him how good He is, how great He is, and how awesome He is.

This is the kind of worship that causes you to humble yourself and bow down to the ground before His presence. It's the kind of worship that you cannot go through in five minutes. It's the kind of worship that you have to forget about who you are and where you are. It's the kind of worship where you have to forget about the time, and immerse yourself into His presence.

When you can worship God like that, He begins to pour in the oil and the wine. He begins to strengthen you, encourage you, and lift you up. There's a song that says, *"we get lifted up, when we lift Him up."* That's exactly what happens when we begin to lift Him up.

You may go down on your knees troubled, crying, depressed, burdened and overwhelmed, but as you lift up your hands and glorify and magnify Him, He pours in His strength. This kind of worship may take a half-hour, an hour, or even several hours of nothing but worshipping God. This is not a time to tell God what you want or need, but a time to focus on Him and worship Him.

When you begin to intimately worship God, your are taking the focus off of you and what you are going through, and placing your focus on the Lord.

Matthew 11:28-30 Come unto me, all ye that labour and are heavy laden, and I will give you rest. Take my yoke upon you, and learn of me; for I am meek and lowly in heart: and ye shall find rest unto your souls. For my yoke is easy, and my burden is light.

When you place your focus on the Lord by worshipping Him, you exchange your burdens and yokes with His. Worship removes the heavy burdens from upon you and places them upon Him. In exchange, you receive His easy and light burdens and yokes of inner peace and strength.

The morning that my mother passed away was perhaps the single most difficult time of my life. As I left the hospital (after the doctor pronounced her death), I returned to her home. As I walked in the door, with tears streaming down my face, all I could say was, "how am I going to make it without my mother?" I wanted to fall apart. I felt like I was about to loose it. Then I remembered seeing something my Bishop, Bishop Nate Holcomb, did years ago after the lost of a friend and member of our church. Upon arriving at the home and coming into the room and seeing the body, he just began to lift up his hands and praise God. For several minutes, he did nothing but magnify, praise and exalt God.

As I remembered this, I then began to do the same thing. I began to lift up my hands and walk through the house praising, glorifying and exalting the Lord. With almost uncontrollable tears, I cried out, **"Lord, you're still God anyway. Even though I didn't get the miracle I had prayed for, You're still the same God who has healed her in the past. You're the same God who has healed me in the past. You're the same God who has been with me, blessed me and provided for me all the days of my life. And, You're the same God that shall continue to be with me. You still have all the power and authority to heal and deliver. And because you didn't heal her this time doesn't stop you from being God. You are still God. You have always been God; and You shall forever more be The Almighty God. And, I shall continue to put my faith and trust in You and in Your awesome Word to save, set free, heal and deliver, all the days of my life."**

I went on like this for quite some time. And, before I knew it, an overwhelming sense of comfort and peace came upon me. I was then able to gather and compose myself and begin focusing on the things I needed to do. As the days and weeks went on, I continued to worship and praise the Lord each day. I continued to spend quality time in praise and worship, getting into that secret place (the Holy of Holies) each morning and at other times throughout the day. As I continued, the Lord gave me the strength and peace I needed. People around me who knew how much I loved my mother were constantly calling me and making sure that I was doing fine. I assured them that the Lord had comforted and strengthened me, and He was peacefully taking me through.

If you are going through a storm, you need to find this *"secret place."* It's not a place that you only visit once; you must *"dwell"* there. Only those who know how to find the secret place of worship (and dwell there) will be sheltered from the effects of the storm. When you learn how to dwell there, you will be able to *"abide"* in a place where you can have *"peace, even in the midst of the storm."*

You dwell there by beginning your day in worship. Before you ask God for anything, you must spend quality time in His presence. Sing songs that glorify, magnify and lift up the Lord. Sing them unto the Lord exalting Him from your heart. Lift your hands unto Him in sacrifice. Bow down before Him in humility.

To dwell there, you don't stop when you end your morning prayer time; you maintain the heart of prayer and worship all throughout the day. This is what the Bible meant in 1 Thessalonians 5:17 when it says, *"Pray without ceasing."* Praying without ceasing does not mean that you do not stop praying. It means that you have a continued attitude of prayer. It's when you take opportunities throughout the day—taking moments to stop and pray.

To hide yourself, you "worship without ceasing." You begin your prayer time worshipping God—making intimate worship a priority in your day and in your prayer time. You take time throughout the day and you worship and praise Him. You spend time in worship with Him not only in the morning, but also in the evening and before you go to sleep at night. It's a continual attitude of worship.

Some people can only worship God for five minutes. While five minutes may be sufficient when you are not in the storm or trouble, when you need to hide yourself from the effects of the storm, you need much more than five minutes. When the devil exalts his attack against you by sending the storm your way, you must find shelter by exalting your worship.

The Good Times

Some cannot experience this type of worship. Most people can only worship God in the good times. Anyone can worship God in the good times. Anyone can worship Him when their finances are good, their job is doing good, and all is well. But God wants to know who can worship Him in the midnight hour—when all hell is breaking loose. He wants to know who can worship Him when the tears are streaming down, and you don't know what to do. This is the time that we are to do like Job and hide ourselves in that secret place of worship.

God is looking for a virtuous bride and not a part-time lover. A part-time lover (girlfriend/boyfriend) is someone who will only be with you as long as everything is going well between the two of you.

Casual dating is not God's plan. It's the world's way of enjoying the benefits of marriage (companionship, intimacy, and sexual relations) without the commitment and binding agreement of marriage. In dating, couples often break up and find someone else when troubles and difficulties between each other arise. However, in marriage, (because of the commitment and the binding agreement of marriage) they tend to stay together and try harder to work through their difficulties.

God is looking for the same thing. He is looking for us to come and worship Him in the bad times—when we're going through the storm, just as we do in the good times when we are being blessed. And, when we can hide ourselves in God through worshiping Him through our troubled times, we can say like Paul said in the midst of his trial: *"I'm troubled on every side, yet not distressed; I am perplexed, but not in despair; persecuted, but not forsaken; cast down, but not destroyed."* We can say this even in the midst of the storm because we are hid in Christ and insulated from the destructive effects of the storm.

When you hide yourself in Him through worship, He may not take you out of the trouble, but He will take you through the trouble. You will find yourself being able to go through the storm and keep your joy and your peace. People around you who may know what you are going through will wonder how you are making it.

They will wonder how you are still able to smile, and still have peace. It will be because—even though you may be in the storm, God has insulated and sheltered you from the effects of the storm, leaving you in peace.

Chapter 5

Get Down in a Low Place

"Hit the Deck"

In a physical storm, once you have found shelter from the storm (meaning a building or structure), the next thing you do is try to find a low place. If at all possible, you should try to find shelter that has a basement, cellar or some sort of underground area. In a storm, such as a hurricane or tornado, there are usually all kinds of objects flying around in the air. In fact, most injuries from storms come from flying debris.

If your structure collapses, you will be more secure in shelter which is below ground. If your place of shelter does not have a basement, cellar or underground area, you need to get as low as you possibly can on the ground or floor. The closer you are to the floor, the less chance you have of being hit by flying debris.

In war, when soldiers hear incoming artillery fire, they yell loudly, "**hit the deck!**" When soldiers hear this warning, they stop wherever they are and immediately get down flat on the ground. The reason they get down is because when a blast occurs, it explodes upwards. If a soldier is standing upright near an artillery or hand grenade explosion when it occurs, they can become injured or killed by the exploding scrap metal or debris from the blast.

Spiritually speaking, the low place represents a place of humility before others. We must first have humility before God. Worship (finding shelter), helps to bring us to a place of true humility before God. Most Christians have no problem with having humility before the Lord, but having humility before man is another thing. To have humility before man is to put others and their needs equal to or above yours.

In Matthew, chapter 28, one of the Pharisees asked Jesus what was the greatest commandment. Jesus responded and told him that the greatest commandment was to *"love the Lord with all your heart, soul, strength and might."* He then went on to tell him that the second greatest commandment was to *"love thy neighbor as thyself."* To spiritually get in a low place, you must come to a place where you become as concerned about your neighbor's needs as you are about yours. This is not man's way of doing things. Man's way is to put self number one (self-preservation). But God's ways are dire metrically opposite to those of man.

Isaiah 55:8-9 For my thoughts are not your thoughts, neither are your ways my ways, saith the LORD. For as the heavens are higher than the earth, so are my ways higher than your ways, and my thoughts than your thoughts.

God doesn't think like man. His ways are not like man's ways. Man's way says, "Be first." God's way says, *"Be last and then you shall be first."* Man's way says, "Look out for number one." God's way says, *"esteem others more highly than yourself."* Man's way says, "seek to be the greatest." God's way says, *"Be a servant, then you shall be the greatest."* Man's way says, "Love yourself first." God's way says, *"Love your neighbor as yourself."* If we are going to follow the Lord, we must change our ways and adapt His ways.

"Hitting the Deck" or getting in a low place is something that is very difficult to do. It's difficult because the natural tendency when we are in a storm is to want people to help us, encourage us, and to strengthen and aid us. We feel like we're the one in need, and we are looking for someone to minister to us.

When people are ministering to us and helping us, that's the upright (or standing) position. This represents the position in battle where the soldier is standing when the artillery round or hand grenade explodes. When the soldiers are upright or standing, they are in perfect position to be injured or killed during the explosion. However, the soldier who "hits the deck" (get down on the ground) is in the best position to survive the blast. We do need people to minister to us while we are going through the storm; but if we simply wallow in our misery, it will bring depression and distress (the upright position). The best position is to "hit the deck."

The way that you spiritually *"hit the deck"* is by retaliating against Satan. If you just sit there in the midst of the storm in your misery, Satan will drain your faith, hope and strength. But when you retaliate (by getting down low or hitting the deck), you gain faith, strength and hope.

The way that you retaliate is by not crawling up in a corner and hiding—waiting on people to minister to you, but rather, by coming out swinging. In a boxing match, if a fighter is on the ropes and all he is doing is covering up, the other fighter will wear him out. The only way for the fighter on the ropes to get the other fighter off him is by punching back, or retaliating.

For Example: You might be sick or someone close to you may be sick or ill. You retaliate (or get in a low place) by finding someone else that is sick and ministering to them. You visit them, encourage them and earnestly pray for them. When you are sick or ill, you will not feel like ministering to others, but you do it anyway because you know that this is how you fight back.

You might be going through marriage difficulties. Retaliate (get in the spiritual low place) by finding someone else that may have marriage or family difficulties and encouraging them and committing their marriage to fervent prayer. Your finances might be under attack. Retaliate by praying for someone else that has financial difficulty. You can even take a step of faith and make a sacrifice to help someone else financially. Even if it's only ten or fifteen dollars, retaliate against the devil by sacrificing and giving something to someone in need. I am a tither and a giver. I believe in giving. But I believe that we don't give to each other enough.

Retaliate against Satan by making a sacrifice and giving to someone. When you retaliate like this, instead of Satan draining you of your faith and strength, you gain strength and faith instead.

*John 4:31-34 **In the mean while his disciples prayed him, saying, Master, eat. But he said unto them, I have meat to eat that ye know not of. Therefore said the disciples one to another, Hath any man brought him ought to eat? Jesus saith unto them, my meat is to do the will of him that sent me, and to finish his work.***

Prior to this passage, Jesus had just finished ministering to *"the woman at the well."* Immediately afterwards, the disciples arrived with food for Jesus and gave to Him to eat. When they urged Him to eat, Jesus responded by saying, *"I have meat to eat that ye know not of."*

Meat has always been one of man's greatest sources of protein and energy or strength. After Jesus said this, His disciples wondered if someone else had come and brought Him food while they were away. Then Jesus—knowing their thoughts, spoke up by saying *"My meat is to do the will of him that sent me, and to finish his work."* In other words, Jesus was saying that He gained supernatural strength and energy in doing the work and will of God.

Again, Jesus had just finished ministering to the woman at the well. Not only did Jesus change her life, but she also went and told the whole town about Jesus, and many of them received Christ. Jesus was, in essence, saying that ministering to this woman gave Him supernatural strength and energy that their natural, carnal minds couldn't understand. His ministry to that woman and to the people of that town energized Him so much that it even took away His natural, physical appetite. I have found this to be true in my life. When I know that I am truly doing the will of God and the work of God, I get a boost of supernatural strength and energy like nothing else.

Anyone who really knows me, know that I love good food. There are very few things that can spoil or take away my appetite when I am hungry. I once worked as a nurse in the army and once worked in an emergency room. I have actually eaten lunch while watching people bleeding and being stitched back together and it didn't bother my appetite at all.

I love to watch nature programs on television, and can eat dinner while watching gruesome scenes and still eat with no problem. However, if I am having dinner with someone and we get into a spiritual uplifting conversation about the goodness of the Lord, and the work of the Lord, it seems that my appetite almost leaves me. As hungry as I may be at that time, talking about the Lord, His goodness and His work, practically takes away my appetite.

When you begin to retaliate against Satan, by praying for and helping others while you are in your storm—like Jesus, it becomes a type of spiritual meat or energy for you. It helps you to gain supernatural spiritual strength, energy and stamina in your life. And instead of Satan draining you and pulling you down, you become uplifted, strengthened and encouraged even in the midst of your storm.

Again, it's fine to have others to minister to you when you are in the storm. But if you stay in that place of misery too long, Satan will try and trap you there and drain you. But when you retaliate (by praying for and helping others), instead of Satan draining you of your joy and strength, you will gain the joy, peace and strength you need to make it through your storm.

Chapter 6

Hold on for Dear Life

W e discovered earlier that the first thing you do in the midst of the spiritual storm is to identify what kind of storm you are facing. The second thing you do, according to Psalm 51:1, is hide yourself in the secret place of God through continual intimate worship. The third thing you do is to get into a low place—a place of humility, by earnestly praying for and helping others. The fourth thing you do is also the same thing you do in a physical storm. You quickly find something that is solid and will not move or give way, preferably something anchored to the ground. You then grab a strong hold on it, and hold on for dear life.

In the midst of a natural storm, people often run to the bathroom and get down low and grab hold to the commode or bathtub. The reason why people do this is because the bathroom plumbing fixtures are often the only items in a house that are anchored in the ground. While the rest of the house is fastened to the floor, the bathroom plumbing goes deep into the ground—anchoring the fixture to the ground.

This is why we have seen, in the aftermath of a tornado that has hit a home, many times the only thing that was left standing was the commode or bathtub. These bathroom fixtures are able to remain standing because the plumbing anchors them down into the ground. So, when everything else is blown away, they are able to still remain standing.

So, the fourth thing we do in a spiritual storm is the same thing we do in a physical storm. We find something that will not be moved or shaken spiritually, and we also hold on to it for dear life. The only thing we know in this world that will not move, be shaken or blown away is the Word of the Living God.

When we go through the storm, we've got to get our soul anchored in the Lord. The way we get our soul anchored in the Lord is by getting it anchored in the Word of God.

Hebrews 11:1 tells us, *"Faith is the substance of things hoped for..."* However, we need something to anchor our faith to our hope. The reason we need something to anchor our faith is because many times our faith becomes unstable. James 1:8 calls it *"double-minded."* To be *double-minded* is to allow your faith to waver. When we are releasing our faith to believe God for something, there are times when our faith is strong; but there are also times when our faith becomes weak and frail.

During these times, our faith is often like a ship on the water that moves with every wind and wave. But when that ship weighs or drops its anchor, it stabilizes that ship and the anchor keeps it from moving. Likewise, with our faith, we need the Word of God to help anchor our faith to our hope (the substance of what we are believing God for).

Is your soul anchored in the Lord? Whatever you have

been turning to in the midst of your storms of life is what your soul is truly anchored *to*. Whether it has been drugs, alcohol, lust, or even a person—whatever it may have been, it has been your anchor. Many people have thought their soul was anchored in the Lord, but in the midst of the storm, they had to lean on a particular person. It's all right to have someone there in your storms to help you, but make sure that your faith is anchored in the Lord and His Word, and not in that person.

How Do We Get Our Soul Anchored?

Psalms 91:1-2 He that dwelleth in the secret place of the most High shall abide under the shadow of the Almighty. "I will say of the LORD," He is my refuge and my fortress: my God; in Him will I trust.

These two verses of scripture show us how we become anchored. David was the writer of the 91st Psalm. In verse two David said, "*I will say of the Lord...*"

We are made of three parts: spirit, soul and body. When we are going through the storm, two of the parts, the soul and the spirit, want to speak through our body. Most of the time we allow our soul to do the talking. In other words, we allow our soul to speak or talk based upon how we feel. If we let our soul do the talking, (which we normally do) our soul will say things such as:

"I don't know how I'm going to make it."

"I'm tired of this job; they can take this job and shove it."

"I'm tired of this woman/man; I want a divorce."

"I can't take this anymore; I need a drink, drugs, etc."

If we allow our soul to do the talking for us, our soul will normally say things based upon how it feels at that moment. There have been many lives destroyed, jobs lost, marriages lost, and other losses because people have reacted in the moment instead of responding in the Spirit.

Don't React, Respond

When all hell breaks loose in your life, don't react, respond. When you experience the storm, you can either react in the flesh or respond in the spirit.

It's like when you are driving on a slippery wet or icy road. If the car begins to skid, most people follow their normal instinctive reaction, which is to immediately hit the brakes. But hitting the brakes, however, only cause you to loose complete control of the vehicle. The correct thing to do if you begin to skid is to try to remain calm and not give in to the natural reaction of hitting the brakes, but respond to the skid by steering your car in the direction of the skid until you gain control.

This is a defensive driving technique that has been taught and re-taught to drivers for years. And yet, as many times as we've heard it, many still fall into the trap of slamming on the brakes when they are caught in a skid.

Spiritually speaking, it's the same way. Like the driver's natural reaction to slam on the brakes in a skid, our natural reaction in a crisis is to react to how we feel by worrying, fretting, fearing, and allowing our soul to talk negatively about our circumstances. When we begin doing this in our storm, we are caught in a spiritual skid and headed for a collision.

Instead of allowing your soul to skid out of control, you must respond in the spirit by doing what David did, *"saying of the Lord."* Like the driver in the skid must respond by directing or steering the car towards the direction of the skid, the way that you *"say of the Lord"* is by steering or directing your mouth to only say what the Lord (the Word of God) says about your situation.

In Proverbs 18:21, the Word of God declares to us that *"death and life are in the power of the tongue."* We must remember to keep this before us continually. We have creative power in our words. We can either skid into deeper trouble by speaking negatively about our situations, or we can gain control of the skid or storm by speaking our way out of our situation (by saying of the Lord).

Jesus never told us to walk by (or react based upon) how we feel, but to walk by our faith. And, the way that we walk by faith is to allow our spirits to do the talking instead of our soul. This is what David meant by when he said, *"I will say of the Lord."* In other words, David was saying that he was not going to say what he felt, but rather, "say of the Lord" (the Word of God) about his situation.

What have you been saying about your circumstances in your storm? Have you been allowing your soul to "react" and say what it feels, or have you been allowing your spirit to "respond" by *"saying of the Lord."*

There are different types of prayers. One of the forms of prayer is confession (confessing the Word of God). Although confession does several things, one of the primary things that confession does is to mold, train and transform the soul.

Romans 12:2 And be not conformed to this world: but be ye transformed by the renewing of your mind, that ye may prove what is that good, and acceptable, and perfect, will of God.

Since we live in the world, we are always being bombarded by the influences of the world. And, if we do not go through a constant transformation, our souls will become conformed to the image of the world. Although we may be saved and going to heaven, we can have a soul that reflects more of the image of the world than the image of Christ. This is why you can have people who attend church regularly and say that they are Christians, but yet their lifestyle reflects more that of a non-Christian than a Christian. It's because there is no transformation of their soul.

The way in which we transform our soul is by *"saying of the Lord."* The more we do this, the more our minds (which is the soul) will become transformed into the image of God, rather than the image of the world, and the more our faith will become stable and anchored to our hope and not blown away in the storm.

The other thing that confession does is to counteract negative circumstances in our lives. As we know, God spoke the world into existence. As born-again believers, He has also given us His authority to change our circumstances by the words we speak. But this divine speaking authority is only effective when we speak His Word. As we confess and speak God's Word, we are using the divine creative authority of God to create and change things in the spiritual realm. As we continue to speak His Word, that in which we have created with our words in the spiritual realm eventually becomes manifested in the natural realm. It is then that our circumstances begin to change and line up with the Word of God that we have been speaking.

The 23rd Psalm

Most of us have read or heard the 23rd Psalm. Most of us also know that David wrote the 23rd Psalm. But what few of us know is "when" David actually wrote this psalm. David didn't write this psalm when he was King of Israel, sitting in his palace with all of his riches and servants. David wrote this psalm when he was in the Judean wilderness being hunted by King Saul.

Saul was King of Israel; but due to his disobedience and rebellion to the will and purpose of God, God anointed David to be the new king in his stead. Although David had done nothing wrong to Saul, Saul (out of jealousy) took a portion of his army and hunted for David day and night to kill him. Saul thought that if he could kill David, he could perhaps keep David from replacing him as king.

David fled to the Judean wilderness in an attempt to escape from Saul and his army. This was truly a storm for David. He had been separated from his family, falsely accused of treason by Saul—a crime punishable by death; and he had to run for his life in a place that was hard, rough and barren.

There was nothing in this wilderness but mountains, caves and rocks. But it was in this place of hardship that David wrote what is perhaps one of the most comforting chapters in the entire book of Psalms. Rather than to allow this crisis to destroy Him in the midst of his storm, David began to get his soul anchored.

He began by saying,

"The Lord is my shepherd, I shall not want."

Again, as we *"say of the Lord"* about our circumstances, we are able to change and counteract circumstances in our lives. When David said, *"the Lord is my shepherd, I shall not want,"* what he was essentially saying was that the Lord is my provider, and he shall supply all my needs. David had many needs there in the wilderness. He had needs for food, water, shelter, and many other things—all of which he had to trust God to provide for him. Therefore, when David said, *"I shall not want,"* he was actually *"saying of the Lord,"* and thus stabilizing and anchoring his faith to his hope. By continually doing this, he changed his situation in the spiritual realm, and they soon changed in the physical realm.

The equivalent scripture of what David said here is found in Philippians 4:19: **"But my God shall supply all your need according to his riches in glory by Christ Jesus."** If the place of your storm is a state of lack, you too can change your state and circumstances by *"saying of the*

Lord" instead of saying the way things look.

"He maketh me to lie down in green pastures"

Green pastures represents not only having your needs met, but having God's abundance. If you are in a state of financial lack, don't just stop with confessing that your needs are met, take a step farther like David did and go ahead and confess that you are walking in God's abundance. The equivalence of this passage is found in Ephesians 3:20: *"Now unto him that is able to do exceeding abundantly above all that we ask or think, according to the power that worketh in us."*

"He leadeth me besides the still waters"

Still waters represent peace. In the natural realm, David didn't have any peace. If you can imagine an army searching for someone in the wilderness, you would also be able to imagine that the person they were searching for would have very little or no rest or peace. They would need to be on the go all the time. They would need to be awake and watchful at all times. They would not be able to get much sleep or rest; therefore, they wouldn't have much peace. But, because David knew how to go through his storm, he was able to achieve inner peace even in the midst of his turmoil. The equivalence of this scripture is found in Philippians 4:7: *"And the peace of God, which passeth all understanding, shall keep your hearts and minds through Christ Jesus."*

When we go through trials in our lives, the world looks at our reaction to our trials. And, it's our reaction to the trials that determine what kind of witness we are to the world. Our reaction will determine whether we are a witness of the inner peace and strength of God, or whether we are a reproach unto the Lord and turn people away from Him. The world is looking for something they do not have. And, when they see us going through a crisis and still keeping the peace of God upon us, it become an attractive witness to them, and can draw them to Christ.

I spent thirteen years in the military. The military is very chaotic at times. One of the things I believed in doing, and still do to this day, was to allow the peace of God to operate in my life. I did this through constantly confessing the Word of God over my life concerning God's peace. It was operating in this peace that allowed me to testify more of Jesus Christ with my life than I could ever do with my lips.

People would come to me all the time and tell me that they didn't know how I made it through all the chaos and still kept my composure and my peace. Of course, that was an instant open door for me to testify now with my lips about Jesus Christ, the Prince of Peace. It's through the storms of life that God shows us off to the world. And, it's His inner peace that becomes a reflection of Jesus Christ, and a lighthouse that points people to Him.

"He resoreth my soul"

When we are going through the storms of life, there are times when we feel like throwing in the towel and giving up. Storms drain us, wear on us, and make us want to give up on our jobs, marriages, finances and other areas of struggle. David also probably wanted to give up in the midst of his storm. But instead of quitting, he continued to rehearse God's Word about his strength. Instead of giving up, David received his strength and prevailed. The equivalent scripture of this passage is found in Psalms 73:26: **"My flesh and my heart faileth: but God is the strength of my heart, and my portion for ever."**

The entire 23rd psalm is a pattern of how David changed his circumstances and made it through his storm. He got his soul anchored in the Lord by *"saying of the Lord."* This is also how we get our soul anchored in the Lord. Whatever you are going through, find the Word of God that applies to your situation and begin to *"say of the Lord."*

Chapter 7

Wait Patiently

In our previous point, we discovered that if a storm hits your house or shelter that you are to find something solid, and "hold on for dear life." While you are holding on, you are to also wait patiently until the storm has passed on before you attempt to emerge from it.

We live in a fast-food, fast-service, and fast-paced society. We want fast food and fast service, and when we are caught in a storm, we even want fast deliverance. There are many times that God does give us quick, precise deliverance from the storm. But there are other times when our deliverance is long and slow. There are some who enter a storm and do all the right things for a week or so—about the time they figure that God should have worked it out for them; but when their storm seem to take longer than expected or anticipated, they become impatient and lose faith in God and fall apart.

There are some storms which we just cannot rush. No matter how much we want to rush God, we can't. If we are caught in a natural storm, the only thing we can do is to wait it out. Likewise, if we are caught in a spiritual storm, the only thing you can do is to also *wait* on the Lord to deliver us.

Psalms 40:1 I waited patiently for the LORD; and he inclined unto me, and heard my cry.

It takes Godly patience to wait upon the Lord's deliverance. Waiting upon the Lord and His deliverance is difficult for most of us. It's difficult because we live in a society that is not accustomed to waiting and being patient. We make many mistakes in life because we don't know how to wait upon the Lord. Many have made the mistake of marrying the wrong person because they did not have the patience to wait upon the Lord. Many have dug themselves in humongous holes and craters of debt because they did not have the patience to wait upon the Lord.

If you are caught in a natural storm, and you attempt to come out of your shelter before the storm has passed, you could become injured or consumed. Likewise, in a spiritual storm, if you don't have the patience to wait upon God's deliverance, you could also become spiritually or emotionally injured or consumed.

If you are caught in a storm, be patient and wait upon the Lord. Movements that you make during the storm could be detrimental to your life. If you are having difficulty waiting upon the Lord, pray (each day) and ask God to give you Godly patience to wait upon Him—and He will. Satan is *"The Deceiver."* And, there is no better time for him to come in our lives and attempt to deceive us than when we are confused and dazed from the storm. During and immediately after the storm we become vulnerable to our emotions. And, it's through this realm of emotions that Satan deceives us into making wrong decisions.

Don't make any major decisions at all until you are out of the storm and can see clearly and distinctively hear from the Lord. Do not move. Do not divorce or marry. Do not buy anything major. Do not quit your job. Do not do anything major in life until you are out of the storm. And, when you do make major decisions after the storm, make sure that you know beyond the shadow of a doubt that you have heard from God.

If you are not positively sure that you are hearing from the Lord, continue to pray and wait upon Him until you are. Some people make hasty decisions during and after the storm, and open the door for Satan to enter and play on their emotions and deceive them into making the wrong decisions—leading them right into another storm. If you must make a major, life-altering decision after a storm, I suggest that you go on a fast. Fasting does several things for us.

One of the things it does for us is to cause us to become sensitive to the voice of the Lord. It helps to move the carnal thinking and reasoning out of the way—allowing us to become sensitive to the true voice of God and His will for our lives. So, before you make major decisions in life, spend quality time in prayer and fasting and get a clear, distinct word from the Lord.

When we can go through the storm and wait patiently for God, He will incline unto us and hear our prayer. But God's deliverance must be in His way and His timing, not ours. As we patiently wait upon Him, even through the long storms, God gives us the strength, endurance, spiritual stamina and peace we need to make it through the storm.

Never Blame God

While you are patiently waiting for your storm to pass over, you should never blame God for the storm. Whether God brought the storm to you, or whether He allowed it to come upon you, "DON'T BLAME GOD!" That's exactly what Satan wants you to do.

Job 1:9-11 Then Satan answered the LORD, and said, Doth Job fear God for nought? Hast not thou made an hedge about him, and about his house, and about all that he hath on every side? thou hast blessed the work of his hands, and his substance is increased in the land. But put forth thine hand now, and touch all that he hath, and he will curse thee to thy face.

Notice the goal of Satan for Job. It was to get Job angry enough with God to curse him. In fact, during the storm, Job's wife—being influenced by Satan, told Job, "*Why don't you just curse God and die?*" This is the same goal that Satan has for us in the storm. We may not go to the extent of cursing God, but if we allow ourselves to blame God and become angry with Him, we will come close to doing the same thing.

Once you become angry with God, Satan will use that anger to turn your heart away from God. Once Satan turns your heart away from God, your spiritual eyes will become blinded, and your heart will then become open and more susceptible to temptation and demonic influence. There are many people who are now bound and in the midst of demonic strongholds because they blamed God for their storms and became angry with Him.

If you are in a storm, never let words of anger towards God come from your mouth. Never let thoughts of anger towards God dwell upon your mind. Don't even entertain these kinds of thoughts for one moment. You may not understand why you are going through the storm. There's an old song that says, *"We'll understand it better by and by."* In other words, we may never understand it all until when we get to heaven. Until then, you must come to a place of faith and trust in the Lord.

This is the place where you have to come to know God as the "Sovereign God"—the God who knows everything; the God who has all things under control; and the God who always has your best interest in mind. If you are going through the storm, you may not understand all the reasons "why" you are going through it, but just have faith in God and trust Him as the Sovereign God.

Glorifying God Through Your Sufferings

While you are waiting for the storm to pass, you can glorify God through your sufferings. God gets glorified in our lives in many ways. We all know that God gets glorified when we testify of Jesus and win the lost to Him. We also know that He gets glorified when we give and we help others.

Most of us are willing vessels to glorify God in these ways. However, there are some that have glorified God by giving their lives—being killed for the gospel of Christ. There are others that may not have been killed, but have suffered torture and abuse—glorifying God. You may never be tortured, and you may never have to give your life for the glory of God, but you can still glorify God just as much if you can go through your storm and keep your faith, trust and love for Him.

Philippians 3:10 *"That I may know him, and the power of his resurrection, and the fellowship of his sufferings...."*

All of us want to know God in the power of His resurrection, which is the demonstration of His power working in and through us; but very few of us want to come to know Him in the fellowship of His sufferings (when we must go through the storms of persecution and sufferings for His glory). When we can go through the storm and keep our faith, love and trust in God, it testifies to others around us of the Lord and gives Him great glory.

Job didn't give his life for the preaching of the gospel. Job was not beaten for testifying of Jesus. But Job glorified God just the same with his faith, trust and patience in God through his storm. Sometimes God simply wants bragging rights. Sometimes God may just want to brag to the devil about your unconditional faith, patience and love for Him like He did Job.

There are some Christians who seem like they have faith and love for God, but their (apparent) faith and love for Him is only based upon their blessings. Look at Job's wife for example. Since Job was a Godly man, I am sure that he married someone who also had a relationship with the Lord. However, after the storm came upon Job's life, his wife abandoned her faith and trust in God. Job's wife represents the level of faith and commitment of many

Christians. As long as God is promptly answering their prayers and meeting their needs, they are anxiously willing to love and serve Him. But when the storm hits their lives (especially in a long storm), like Job's wife, they abandon their faith.

Which type of Christian are you? Are you like Job (willing to remain faithful and love, serve and bring Him Glory even through your sufferings), or Job's wife (only willing to remain faithful to Him as long as everything is going good)? God loves us unconditionally, and He gets glory from those who are also willing to love and trust Him unconditionally.

The Bible says, "*Without faith, it is impossible to please God.*" Many people think that faith is simply believing in God for a blessing or a miracle. While these are types of faith, I believe the kind of faith that God is talking about is the kind of faith in which we are willing to believe and trust in Him independent of the longevity or outcome of our storm. In the midst of Job's trial, he said, "*Though He slay me, yet will I trust Him.*" Job was saying that no matter what happened, or no matter what the outcome was, he was still willing to serve and trust in God. This is the kind of faith and trust in God we must possess if we are going to please Him and bring Him glory.

Just because God doesn't always answer our prayers in the way and manner we think He should, doesn't mean that God hasn't heard our prayers. Prior to Jesus going to the cross, He prayed, "*Father, let this cup pass from before me.*" In other words, Jesus was asking God if it could be done another way. But after He continued to pray, He bent

His will to the Will of God and said, "***Nevertheless, not my will, but thy will be done***." The way in which you go through your storm can either give God glory, honor and praise, or it can bring Him shame and displeasure. Make up in your mind that no matter how long the storm, what kind of storm it is, or the outcome, that you are determined to keep your faith, love and trust in God, and bring Him glory through your storm.

Chapter 8

Keep Moving

P reviously, we discovered that if the storm does hit your building, that you are to wait patiently until the storm has passed. But if it has hit your building, there may be a lot of rubble piled on top of and covering you. In the aftermath of a destructive tornado or hurricane, it sometimes takes hours and even days for volunteers and workers to dig out victims trapped under rubble and debris. The workers will be trying to dig the victims out from the outside, but those that are trapped must also continue to work to dig their way out and break free.

Being buried under rubble and debris is very stressful, fatiguing and wearisome. Because it is so difficult to dig a way out, many just wait and hope that someone will find them and eventually dig them out. The problem with that is they never know the extent of damage on the outside. The damage could be so widespread and extensive, that it could take days before workers and volunteers actually get to them.

Therefore, it is recommended that you (as much as you are possibly able) dig your way out. Try to find some way of escape. If you cannot dig your way out, it is recommended that you attempt to locate something that you can knock on and make noise, such as a metal pipe. Keep knocking on it until you are sure that someone hears you, and knows you are there. Don't assume that someone will find you. Keep moving, if possible, and keep knocking and making noise.

In chapter two, "The Purpose of the Storm," we gave an analogy about the spider and the fly. In my study of spiders, I found that some of the small insects that get caught in the spider's web actually get away. What happens is that the spider often gets to them and injects them with its paralyzing venom before they can escape. But if the insect can just keep moving and keep fighting to get free, and not allow the stickiness of the web to tire it out, the insect has a chance of escaping.

When you are going though the storm, you must (like the insect caught in the spider's web) keep moving until you break free. Don't sit there, waiting for your storm of adversity to paralyze you with its venom of depression, distress and hopelessness. When you keep moving, keep knocking and keep fighting, you will become encouraged and uplifted instead of becoming depressed or distressed.

Keep Moving by Keeping on Praying

Another way we keep moving is to keep praying. Our soul is like a child. Children are not disciplined to do things they need to do. Parents must take the oversight of their children to assure needful things are carried out—because children only want to do things based upon how they feel. When you go through the storm, your soul may want to revert back to a childlike attitude concerning prayer. Since your soul is under distress, you may not feel like praying. It's not your spirit that does not want to pray, it's your flesh being motivated by your soul that is fighting against your spirit. Jesus said, regarding his struggle, ***"The spirit indeed is willing, but the flesh is weak."*** Your spirit knows that you need to pray in the storm. It wants to pray. However, because the soul has been wounded through the storm, it doesn't want to pray. And if you give in to this temptation of prayerlessness, you may become stung. Just as parents must enforce needful things upon their children, we must also enforce and discipline our soul to pray (even when it does not feel like praying).

Prayer sometimes works like a drained battery. If you were to turn your car off and leave your headlights on for several hours, it would drain your car battery. If you attempted to start the car with the drained battery, it would not start. But if you got a jump-start from another power source, it would help to give it the power boost it needs to start the car. Once the battery has been jump-started, the alternator then takes over and continues to run the car, and at the same time recharges the battery.

When you are going through the storm, your prayer life becomes somewhat like the drained battery—sometimes needing a jump-start. I encourage everyone to have a prayer handbook such as, "The Weapons of Our Warfare" and other good prayer handbooks. During those times when your soul doesn't want to pray, begin utilizing your prayer handbooks.

As you begin to read the prayers in the book, it may seem like they are just empty, vain words coming from your mouth. But after a few minutes of praying from the book, your spirit will get ignited and engage, or jump-start your soul. And soon, you will shift into your prayer gear. You will no longer be praying mere words from your lips, but powerful anointed words from your heart.

Don't allow your soul the unaffordable luxury of taking prayer time off during the storm (simply because it doesn't feel like praying). Jump-start your prayer time off every day if necessary. Whatever you have to do to keep your prayer life moving—do it, and you will not get stuck in the spider's web.

Keep Moving by Keeping Your Mind Moving

As we discovered in chapter three, during the storm your soul will begin to look for alternate ways of escape. Instead of escaping to the shelter of the Lord, it will begin looking for carnal shelters like those we named earlier, such as alcohol, drugs, sex, sexual affairs and perversions, as well as others. You must keep your mind moving and combat the soul's thirst for these sinful forms of shelter.

Keep moving by continuing to go to church. During the storm, Satan will give you all kinds of excuses why you don't need to go to church. And, your injured soul will be more than willing to accept almost any reason that Satan gives you to stay at home. During the storm, more than any other time, you need to go to church to hear the Word of God, worship the Lord, and fellowship with the saints of God. Each of these three things will help give you strength and encouragement through your storm. When Satan whispers in your ear and tells you that you are tired and you need to stay at home, tell yourself, "I'm going to the house of the Lord." Don't allow yourself to sit at home on church days watching television—keep moving by going to the house of the Lord.

While in the storm, you need to be cautious about what type of television programs and movies you watch. If you watch the wrong type of programs and movies, Satan will use them to subliminally speak to your soul. It's hard enough keeping negative influences of the world out of your spirit when you are not in the storm. But if you are in the storm, it becomes much more dangerous.

It's dangerous because during the storm, your soul is injured and more vulnerable to receive the sinful suggestions you are bombarded with by Satan with the wrong shows. If you watch the wrong programs, you will find yourself desiring things that you know are wrong. Satan will give you the excuse that you need a break, and propose that you use the sinful suggestions you receive from negative programs to take that break.

Keep your mind moving by watching as many Christian television programs as you can. Watch programs that encourage you and lift you up. Listen to music that is uplifting and make you think about the Lord, instead of the kind that makes you want to dance. Listen to as many cassette taped messages as you can. Read the Word of God as much as you can.

These things will persuade you to seek shelter in the Lord, while negative television programs, movies and music will persuade you to seek shelter in sin. If you are in a prolonged storm, you still need to be cautious about what type of programs you are watching. When you know that a movie or television program is rated "R," then you already know that it may obtain some challenging temptations and seductive issues for your soul. Again, if you watch other than Christian programming, try to watch something that will not lure you to seek shelter in sin or something destructive to your soul.

Chapter 9

Encourage Yourself

W e said earlier that if you are caught in a natural storm and the storm hits your building, if you are buried under rubble, you must keep moving and keep knocking. While you are continuing to move and break free of the rubble, you must encourage yourself. When you encourage yourself, you keep discouragement from taking hold of you.

Another encouraging example of David weathering his storm of adversity is found in 1 Samuel Chapter 30. In the process of David fleeing from Saul, he had banded together with his own small army of warriors. Other men who were like David, distressed and running from something, joined themselves with him.

To escape Saul's constant pursuit, David fled into the land of the Philistines. He and his men joined themselves, and were accepted by the Philistines. David, his men and their families were camped in a town called Ziglag. While they were away from their camp one day, the Amalekites raided the camp and took off with David's family, his men's families and all they possessed. When David and his men returned, they found that the town had been burned to the ground and everything was gone. In one instance, his wives, children, home, and all his possessions were gone. To make matters worse, David's men blamed him, and began talking about stoning him for it. At first, he bitterly cried and became depressed and distressed over this grave loss. But the Bible says that he did something profound. In the midst of this storm of doom and gloom, "he encouraged himself."

1 Samuel 30:6   And David was greatly distressed; for the people spake of stoning him, because the soul of all the people was grieved, every man for his sons and for his daughters: "but David encouraged himself in the LORD his God."

The Bible is not clear on how he encouraged himself, but it did say that he encouraged himself *"in the Lord."* I believe that he encouraged himself the same way he had done in his other adversity, by *"saying of the Lord."* Instead of wallowing in his distress, I believe that David got alone and began to do what he had done before: worshipping God, praying and confessing the Word of God, and confessing God's ability to bring him through. If he had done these things in the wilderness when he was alone being hunted by Saul and his army, why wouldn't he do it now?

The way you encourage yourself in the Lord is by the following:

1. Change your focus
2. Tell yourself you're going to make it
3. Rehearse your past victories and testimonies
4. Magnify the Lord and His greatness

5. Don't allow the devil to steal your vision—see yourself coming out of the storm.

Change Your Focus

Philippians 3:13-14 Brethren, I count not myself to have apprehended: but this one thing I do, forgetting those things which are behind, and reaching forth unto those things which are before; I press toward the mark for the prize of the high calling of God in Christ Jesus.

When you are in the midst of your storm, you must *"forget"* (stop focusing on) how bad things look for you now, and begin focusing on how things will be, according to your confession. The 23rd Psalm was not a confession of David's present circumstances at the time of his confession, but rather, a confession of faith (of how he desired them to be according to the Word of God). Don't allow your mouth to even speak of your negative circumstances. Don't allow your mind to sit idle dwelling upon them. Keep moving by pressing forward in your words and thoughts to your place of deliverance.

Tell Yourself That You're Going to Make It

Begin telling yourself that you're going to make it. Satan will speak nothing but failure, defeat and despair to your mind. Don't let the devil do all the talking to you. Talk back to your soul and keep moving. Encourage yourself in the Lord by telling yourself, **"I'm going to make it through this storm!"** When you wake up in the morning, tell yourself, "I'm going to make it through this storm!" When tears are streaming down your face, tell yourself, "I'm going to make it through." Throughout the day, week, month, or however long it takes, continue to speak to your soul and keep saying, "I'm going to make it through." Before you begin your day and before you end your day, tell yourself, "I'm going to make it through." The more you say and confess it, the more your soul will begin to believe it. The more your soul becomes transformed to it, the more faith and confidence you will have to make it through.

Rehearse Your Past Victories and Testimonies

Rehearse past testimonies of how God has brought you through in the past. Before David fought Goliath, he rehearsed past testimonies of how God gave him a mighty, personal victory when he fought the lion and the bear. These two testimonies gave him faith and confidence—that as God had delivered him in times past, He was also able to deliver him now.

This is what is meant by Revelation 12:11, *"And they overcame him (Satan) by the blood of the Lamb, and by the Word of their testimony..."* When you begin to testify of victories that God has given you in the past, it increases your faith to believe that God will give you victory over your present crisis. No matter how small or great, or how old or recent your testimony, begin rehearsing them.

2 Chronicles 20:5-8 And Jehoshaphat stood in the congregation of Judah and Jerusalem, in the house of the LORD, before the newcourt, and said, O LORD God of our fathers, art not thou God in heaven? And rulest not thou over all the kingdoms of the heathen? And in thine hand is there not power and might, so that none is able to withstand thee? Art not thou our God, who didst drive out the inhabitants of this land before thy people Israel, and gavest it to the seed of Abraham thy friend for ever? And they dwelt therein, and have built thee a sanctuary therein for thy name?"

In this chapter, Jehoshaphat and his people were surrounded and greatly outnumbered by four armies. When Jehoshaphat gathered his people together, he began to cry out to the Lord on behalf of his people. He rehearsed to God what God had done for his people in the past. He rehearsed the mighty victories that God had given them, and how He had brought them through.

When you go through the storm, keep moving by doing like Jehoshaphat and rehearsing to God how He has brought you through in times past. Get alone with God and rehearse with Him how He delivered you financially. Rehearse to God how He has healed you in the past. Rehearse to Him of occasions when He brought you through past trials and storms. Remind yourself that *"God is the same today, yesterday and forever more."* And, just as He has delivered and brought you through past trials and storms, that He is still able to bring you through your current storm.

Most of us know the end result of this story. The Lord caused confusion to fall upon the opposing armies, and they ended up destroying each other. God gave Jehoshaphat a mighty victory. And, if you can keep moving by rehearsing your past victories, you can also come through your storm victorious.

Magnify the Lord and His Greatness

As long as you look at and focus on your problems, they will begin to look bigger than your God. But when you begin to magnify God, He will begin to look bigger than your problems. If you look at the previous scripture passage, you will find that the first thing he did was to magnify the Lord and His greatness.

When the Children of Israel went to spy out the Promised Land, they sent in twelve spies. Ten of them saw one thing, and two of them saw something completely different. The men who brought back the evil report said that they were not able to take the land.

They reported to Moses that there were giants in the land, and they saw themselves as grasshoppers in the sight of the giants. Joshua and Caleb saw something entirely different. They said, *"We are more than able to conquer them; they are bread for us; and we are well able to overtake the land."* How could the same men see the exact same thing and come out with two entirely different reports? It was because of what they magnified.

The men against them may have been men of great stature. But Joshua and Caleb remembered how God divined the Red Sea and brought them across on dry land. They thought about how God had fed them manna from heaven and rained down quail in the desert. They began to magnify God's greatness. As they magnified God, God became greater than their adversity, and they had faith and confidence to believe that God would perform His Word and give them the victory.

When you magnify God's greatness, the same will happen to you. As you magnify Him, God will begin to look bigger than your problem instead of your problem looking bigger than God's ability. Quit magnifying the bigness of your problem. Begin magnifying the bigness of your God. When you do, you will begin to speak like Joshua and Caleb with faith and boldness and say, "God is well able to bring me through." Magnify God's ability to bring you through. Talk about God's greatness and His ability to restore unto you what the devil has tried to destroy.

Begin to See Yourself Coming Out of the Storm—"Keep Your Vision"

2 Corinthians 4:18   While we look not at the things which are seen, but at the things which are not seen: for the things which are seen are temporal; but the things which are not seen are eternal.

This scripture shows us how we are to keep our vision. Don't allow your vision to focus on how things presently look in your natural, physical circumstances. Change your vision and begin to focus and see yourself out of the storm and in the blessings of the Lord. If you are sick, stop focusing on your sickness and begin to see or envision yourself healed and in good health. If you are broke, stop focusing on how broke you are and begin to focus your vision to see yourself blessed and prosperous.

You may even be in a situation like David in 1 Samuel Chapter 30. You may have lost some things in your life. You may have lost your job, business, car, home, marriage, relatives, friends or any number of things.

In a war, there are times that soldiers have to retreat in battle. Soldiers are taught that they never retreat to surrender; they only retreat to regroup. If you have lost something, and you give up and allow depression to set in, you are retreating to surrender. But if you encourage yourself (in the midst of your loss), you are retreating to regroup.

You must see your retreat only as a setback for a comeback. You must see yourself regaining what you had before. If it's a job you've lost, begin to see yourself getting a better job. If it's a car or home you've lost, begin seeing yourself with a better car or home than you had before. As David encouraged himself, he could see himself regaining what he had lost.

Even when David was being chased by Saul, I believe that he kept his vision alive of the prophecy that he would one day be King of Israel. I believe that no matter how long it took, or how hard his journey was, he never took his eyes off his vision. It is imperative that you get a vision and begin to "see" what you are believing God for, and keep your eyes on your vision.

Because David encouraged himself, he not only regained what he had lost, but he also gained much more. David and his men not only recovered what the Amalekites had taken from them, but they also gained the Amalekites possessions. And if you can keep your focus and your vision, you too can recover not only what the devil has stolen from you, but much more.

Your confession will directly affect your faith, focus and your vision. Whatever you say or confess by faith is what you will see. The more you confess and say, the more you will see. As we confess the Word of God, it will do two things: It will restore our vision and build faith back into our hearts to receive. That's why the scripture tells us that *"faith cometh by hearing."* When we speak and hear the Word of God in our storm, our vision will come alive and become clearer.

This is why the Word of God tells us in Proverbs 29:18, *"Where there is no vision, the people perish."* If you cannot get and keep a vision for your deliverance and blessings, Satan will be able to attack your faith, and thus assassinate your hope to receive the substance and evidence of your deliverance and blessings. But when you confess the Word of God in your storm, it keeps your faith and vision alive to receive your blessings and deliverance.

I believe that each day David was in the wilderness, he could see himself as king, sitting on the throne. I believe that no matter how bad things became, he never forgot or lost his vision. And, because he never lost his vision, he was able to receive the promise of his blessings. No matter how things look for you in the natural, keep your vision. No matter how long it takes, and no matter how things look in the natural, keep seeing yourself out of your storm and in your blessed place. If you are in a storm, you must not only worship your way out and speak your way out, but you must also "see" or envision your way out. And, whatever you are able to see (by revelation and faith in the spiritual realm) you will be able to eventually receive and possess in the natural realm.

These five points are how David encouraged himself in the Lord. This is how we also encourage ourselves in the Lord when all hell breaks loose in our lives. And, just as

David weathered his storm and received the blessings of the Lord, you will also be able to weather your storm and receive your blessings.

Your storm may take you a few days, weeks, months, or even longer. But no matter how long it takes, follow these procedures, and make up in your mind that you are going to keep moving, and you are going to make it through. When all hell breaks loose in your life, you can weather the storm.

Closing Chapter

The Tamer

In closing, I want to give a story that I believe to be very applicable to this message. From what I've been told, the story is true. One day a circus came to a particular town. One of the featured acts in this circus was the world-renowned Bengal tiger. The amazing thing about this tiger is how well it is able to see in the dark. It rests in the day and hunts at night. It uses its excellent night vision to hunt down and capture its prey.

Inside a large cage, the tamer was making these huge man-eating Bengal tigers do all kinds of tricks. Then all of a sudden, the lights went out under the big tent. The people suddenly began to yell and scream for fear of the man who was locked in the cage with these tigers. The ringmaster then attempted to still and quiet the people as best as he could, but still, they were fearful for the life of the tamer.

After several minutes of frantic worry over the man's life, the lights finally came back on, and to the amazement of the audience, the tamer was fine. He then finished his act and made his exit from the large cage. The ringmaster then brought the tamer to the center of the ring and asked him how he survived in the cage with those tigers when the lights went out. The tamer responded by saying that he knew that he couldn't see anything at all; and he knew beyond the shadow of a doubt that the Bengal tigers could see him very well. However, he expressed that the way that he made it through those dark moments was to do what he had always done while performing his act. He said, "I didn't stop performing. I simply continued to **crack the whip, and speak with authority**" even in the dark.

When all hell breaks loose in your life, you may feel much like this tiger tamer did when the lights went out. But the way you make it through your storms and dark times is the same way the tamer made it through his dark times. You do it by continuing to "crack the whip (of the Word of God) and speak (the Word) with authority" in your storm and dark times. You must also continue to apply these principles to your life:

1. Recognize what type of storm you are in— Persecution or Prosecution
2. Find Shelter—a place of continual worship and praise
3. Get into a low place—help and pray for others in crisis
4. Find something anchored, and hold on to it for dear life—get your soul anchored by "saying of the Lord"
5. Wait patiently until the storm has passed
6. Keep moving
7. Encourage Yourself

When the rains, floods and storms come against your house, how will you respond? Will you fall apart, or will you stand? Just as people survive natural storms, if you follow these principles, you will be able to also survive the spiritual storm, *"when all hell breaks loose."*

About Spiritual Warfare Ministries

Spiritual Warfare Ministries is an intercessory prayer and teaching ministry assisting the body of Christ through teaching the effective, fervent warfare of Prayer. Our desire is to help teach and train believers and Prayer Warriors in the Kingdom of God to be more victorious and availing in their everyday walk with the Lord, Jesus Christ through prayer.

In Hosea 4:6 God said, *"my people are destroyed because of a lack of knowledge."* We believe that it is a lack of knowledge of how to strategically use and pray the authority of God's Word in prayer warfare that causes the failure and destruction of many Christian lives.

God has anointed Evangelist Scott to teach God's people this knowledge through teaching them the proper principles, rules and precepts of prayer. Evangelist Scott teaches the believer how to pray spiritually aggressive prayer, according to God's Word, which enables them to obtain victory in their lives and gives them the knowledge, authority and boldness to take back, as well as maintain those things that Satan has stolen from them.

(96)

Evangelist Scott and his wife, Doris, have been married for 18 years. They work together in ministry and both have the same heart and passion for prayer, intercession and the desire to see God's people delivered, set free and loosed from the strongholds and clutches of Satan.

We invite you to take advantage of the ministry teaching and preaching of Author and Evangelist Kenneth Scott. You may contact him at the information on the last page. As you hear him speak under the authority and anointing of the Holy Spirit, your life will never be the same again.

* Note: You may also take advantage of the Spiritual Warfare Ministries monthly newsletter, containing enlightening news and information about prayer and other topics that will bless your life. If interested, contact us at the information on the last page.

Other Books and Materials
By Kenneth Scott

The Weapons Of Our Warfare, Volume 1
If you have enjoyed Volume II, then you need volume I. It is a personal handbook of Prayers for your home, marriage, family and many personal issues that we face in our lives each day.

The Weapons Of Our Warfare, Volume 2
If You have enjoyed Volume I, then you need volume II. It is a sequel of volume I, and brings the prayer warrior into the ministry is intercession. A list of prayers that are included in volume II can be found in this enclosure. *Now Available*

The Weapons Of Our Warfare, Volume 3
—Confessing God's Word Over Your Life.
There is a difference between prayer and confession. This book gives the believer understanding in confessions and what they do in your life. It also contain daily confessions for major areas of your life. If you have Volume 1 & 2, then you need volume 3 also. *Coming May, 2002*

The Weapons Of Our Warfare, Volume 4
—Prayers for Children and Teenagers
Children and teenagers have different needs than adults. These prayers are structured on their level, and prepared to meet their needs. This book is a "must" for your children. *Coming June 2002*

The Weapons Of Our Warfare, Spanish Edition
Coming in September 2002

The Weapons Of Our Warfare on Audio Cassette Tapes
Meditate on the anointed Word of God as it is prayed on audio cassette tapes. These tapes contain prayers from volume 1 & 2. There is also a healing tape with the healing prayer, along with over 70 healing scriptures. As You hear these prayers prayed, you can stand in the spirit of agreement and apply them in the spirit to your life, situations and circumstances as you ride in your car, or as you sit in your home. These tapes are a must for every Christian library. *Now Available*

Understanding Your Divine Authority In Prayer

Many Christians are hindered and defeated by Satan simply because they do not know the dominion and authority they have in Christ. This book teaches the believer how to bind and loose Satan and demon spirits, and how to pray and walk in our divine authority. *Now Available*

The Keys To The Kingdom

The Keys To The Kingdom is a wealth of full scriptures to aid and assist the believer in finding the right scriptures for prayer, confessions, study, and meditation for just about every need. *Now Avail.*

Understanding The Lord's Prayer

Just about all of us have prayed "The Lord's Prayer," and even know The Lord's prayer by memory. But very few of us really understand the depths of what Jesus was truly teaching His disciples in this prayer outline. This book gives the believer a scripture by scripture breakdown of this prayer and gives illumination and insight on its understanding. *Coming in July, 2002*

The Principles of Prayer

Jesus said that we have not (what we are praying for) because we ask not. He also said that some of us do ask (in prayer) but we "ask amiss" (the wrong way). There is a right way and a wrong way to pray. This book gives the believer the proper principles and precepts of prayer according to scripture so that your prayers may become effective and strike the mark for what you are praying.
Coming June, 2002

Standing In The Gap

This book teaches the believer the ministry of intercession. As Christians, interceding for one another is not a choice, but a commandment. In fact, if we fail to do so, it is actually a sin. Find out more about our role as intercessors, making up the hedge and standing in the gap for others. *Coming in September, 2002*

Decreeing your Healing — Mini-booklet

This mini-booklet conveniently has the healing prayer, along with the full scriptures passage of over 70 healing scriptures. It is great to either have yourself in case you come under physical attack, or to share with others you have prayed for. *Now Available*

Contact Us:

For prayer requests, questions or comments, write to:

Spiritual Warfare Ministries
Attention: Kenneth Scott
P.O. Box 2024
Birmingham, Alabama 35201-2024

(205) 853-9509

Web Site: www.spiritualwarfare.cc
email us at sprwarfare@aol.com

This book is not available in all bookstores. To order additional copies of this book, please send $7.99 plus $1.80 shipping and handling to the above address.

God has anointed Evangelist Scott to teach and preach on the power of prayer. If you are interested in him coming to minister at your church or organization, please contact him at the information above.